Ways into Science

Growing Plants

Written by Peter Riley

W
FRANKLIN WATTS
LONDON • SYDNEY

First published in 2001 by Franklin Watts
338 Euston Road, London NW1 3BH

Franklin Watts Australia
Level 17/207 Kent Street
Sydney, NSW 2000

Copyrigh
Copyright i   03

Serie
Art
D
Photog
otherwise credited)

A CIP catalogue record for this book
is available from the British Library

ISBN 978 0 7496 7681 0

Printed in Malaysia

Picture Credits:
Chris Fairclough p. 16b; Graham Kitching/Ecoscene p. 14cl;
G.W. Miller/A-Z Botanical Collection p. 16tl; Diana Morris/
Photogenes p. 7; M. Nimmo/FLPA p. 13b; Robert Pickett/
Papilio p. 10b; Dr. Eckhart Pott/Bruce Coleman Collection p.
9b; Iain Sarjeant/Bruce Coleman Collection p. 14cr

Thanks to our models:
Amber Barkhouse, Reece Calvert, Shani-e Cox,
Chantelle Daniel, Ammar Duffus, Alex Green,
Harry Johal and Emily Scott

To my granddaughter Megan Kate.

Franklin Watts is a division of Hachette Children's Books.

Contents

There are all sorts of plants.

A fern plant has large leaves that look like feathers.

The moss plant has tiny leaves.

6

Many plants grow flowers
that have bright colours.

Trees and bushes are plants
that are woody.

Point to the trees, bushes and
flowers in this picture.

The parts of a plant

Here are the parts of a plant that has flowers.

Flowers

Leaves

Stem

Roots

Some plants do not have flowers.

Ferns have brown patches under their leaves instead of flowers.

Some trees have cones instead of flowers.

Roots

Roots grow underground. They take up water from the soil.

This tree has thick roots made of wood. They help to hold the tree in the soil.

This plant has been growing in its pot for a long time.

The root has grown round and round inside the pot. It is 'pot bound'.

The plant must be put in a larger pot. This is called repotting.

Stems

The stem holds up the leaves and flowers.

Some plants have only a few stems.

Some plants have lots.

Some plants have stems that are hidden by the leaves.

12

A tree has a woody stem called a trunk. It is covered in bark.

Every year a tree makes a new thin ring of wood in its trunk.

Do you think this tree is older or younger than you?

Leaves

Leaves have different shapes, colours and sizes.

Some trees lose their leaves in the autumn and grow new ones in spring.

Some trees keep their leaves all year round.

Flowers

Some plants
have lots of
little flowers.

Some plants have
one large flower.

The coloured parts
of a flower are
called the petals.
How many petals
has this flower got?

What forms inside
the flower? Turn
the page to find out.

Seeds

The seeds form inside the flowers. Seeds grow into flowering plants.

Some seeds grow in fruits. They are called pips.

Some seeds grow in pods.

Seeds from different plants don't look the same. They may be different sizes, shapes and colours.

pea

broad bean

mango

sunflower

pumpkin

peach

mung bean

Where are the seeds in this fruit?

17

Planting seeds

Laura and Sam are planting seeds.

They put soil into pots.

They make four holes.

They put a pea seed in each hole.

They cover the seeds with soil.

Sam waters his seeds.

Laura does not water her seeds.

What do you think will happen after a few days?

Turn the page to find out.

Seedlings

Sam's seeds have grown stems and roots. They are called seedlings.

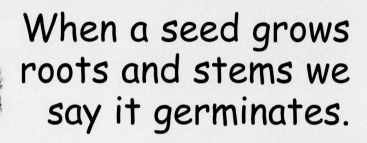

When a seed grows roots and stems we say it germinates.

Laura's seeds have not grown roots or a stem. Why do you think they have not germinated?

Plants and water

This plant has not been watered. Its leaves have drooped. It has wilted.

Nicole waters the plant.

After a few hours the plant stops wilting.

21

Too much water

Too much
water harms
plants.

Do not water
a plant if the
soil feels wet.

Give a plant a small amount of
water if the soil feels dry.

Do the houseplants in your
home need watering?

Nicole and Matthew have cress seedlings.

Nicole puts her seedlings in a place with plenty of light.

Matthew puts his seedlings in a dark place.

What do you think will happen in a few days? Turn over to find out.

Light tests

Nicole's seedlings have grown into plants with dark green leaves and short, firm stems.

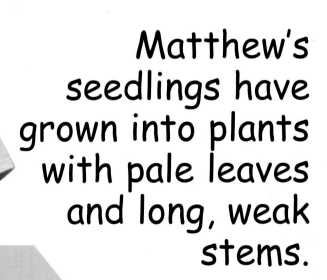

Matthew's seedlings have grown into plants with pale leaves and long, weak stems.

Try this test with some other kinds of seeds.

Sam sets up a test to see if plants grow towards the light.

Cover with hole cut on one side.

He leaves the cover over the plants for a few days. This is how they look.

What does Sam's test show?

Plants we eat

Most of our food comes from plants.

We eat the flowers and stems of the broccoli plant.

We eat the leaves of the lettuce plant.

Oranges are the fruit of orange trees.

Carrots are roots from carrot plants.

Peas are the seeds of the pea plant.

Bread is made from the seeds of the wheat plant.

Make a chart like this and find out which part of the plant people eat.

	root	leaf	stem	flower	seed	fruit
Turnip						
Apple tree						
Tomato plant						
Sunflower						
Cabbage						

Useful words

bark – the covering on a tree.

flower – the parts of the plant where seeds are made. Flowers come in all shapes, sizes and colours.

fruit - the part of the plant that contains its seeds and is often eaten.

germinate – when a seed germinates it makes a stem and roots, which can eventually grow into a plant.

houseplant – plants that are grown in pots and kept indoors.

leaf – a flat, usually green, part of a plant that grows from the stem.

pip – the seed of the flower when it grows in the middle of the fruit.

root – the part of the plant that goes down into the soil to collect water. It also holds the plant firmly in the ground.

seed – plants start out as seeds.

seedling – a young plant that has just started to grow from the seed.

stem – the part of the plant which is usually long and thin. Roots grow from the stem under the ground, and leaves grow from the stem above ground.

trunk – the thick stem of a tree.

Some answers

Here are some answers to the questions we have asked in this book. Don't worry if you had some different answers to ours: you may be right, too. Talk through your answers with other people and see if you can explain why they are right.

Page 13 The tree trunk has more than 30 rings, which means the tree is more than 30 years old.

Page 15 The flower has got six petals.

Page 17 The seeds cannot be seen here. They are called pips and are found at the centre of the apple.

Page 20 The seeds have not germinated because they did not have any water. Seeds need water and warmth to germinate.

Page 22 This will depend on your houseplants. Check the soil every few days to see if it's dry.

Page 25 Sam's test shows that the plants grow towards the light. If you put a pot plant such as a geranium on a sunny windowsill its stems will grow towards the glass.

Page 27 We eat:
The root of a turnip plant.
The fruit of an apple tree.
The fruit of a tomato plant (although it is sometimes called a salad vegetable). Only the fruit of the tomato plant is edible. Other parts are poisonous.
The seed of a sunflower.
The leaves of a cabbage.

Index

About this book

Ways into Science is designed to encourage children to begin to think about their everyday world in a scientific way, examining cause and effect through close observation, recording their results and discussing what they have seen. Here are some pointers to gain maximum use from **Growing Plants**.

• Working through this book will introduce the basic concepts related to growing plants and also some of the language structures and vocabulary associated with them. This will prepare the child for more formal work later in the school curriculum.

• On pages 19 and 23 the children are invited to predict the results of a particular action or test. Ensure that you discuss the reason for any answer they give in some depth before turning over the page. In answering the question on page 19 look for an answer about how the seeds without water will not grow because plants need water to grow. The process of a plant growing from a seed is called germination and this process also requires water. In answering the question on page 23 look for an answer about plants needing light to stay healthy. They actually use light to make food in their leaves.

• You may like to extend the work on page 7 by letting the children look at a collection of houseplants and group them according to whether they have flowers or not and also by the colours of their flowers.

• The work on page 9 could be extended by drying some cones so that they open, then letting the children shake out the seeds.